LOVERS'
WEEKEND GUIDE

ANNE HOOPER

LOVERS' WEEKEND GUIDE

ANNE HOOPER

London, New York, Munich, Melbourne, and Delhi

Designed and edited by
Cooling Brown

Category Publisher **Corinne Roberts**
Senior Managing Art Editor **Lynne Brown**
Senior Editor **Peter Jones**
US Editor **Margaret Parrish**
Senior Designer **Rosamund Saunders**
Designer **Carla De Abreu**
DTP **Karen Constanti**
Production **Kevin Ward**
Jacket Editor **Beth Apple**
Jacket Designer **Neal Cobourne**

First American Edition, 2003
03 04 05 06 07 08 10 9 8 7 6 5 4 3 2 1

Published in the United States by DK Publishing, Inc.
375 Hudson Street
New York, New York 10014

A Cataloging-in-Publication record for this book is
available from the Library of Congress.

ISBN 0-7894-9681-X

Reproduced in Italy by GRB, Italy
Printed and bound by Graphicom, Italy

See our complete product line at
www.dk.com

Introduction

Who needs a lovers' weekend? Answer: every one of us. We need it to celebrate the joy of falling in love; the delight of sexual expression; the intimacy of body on body, and flesh on flesh. We may also need it because everyday life has become stressed, or mundane, or de-eroticized. To *carve out time specifically for lovemaking*, which is what a lovers' weekend entails, is to make an important statement. It says to your partner, "You are really dear to me. I value you enough to take time out especially for you. I want you to myself so that we can have a *fabulous time together*." This, surely, is what most men and women want to hear. I know I do.

Getting away from it all

Yes, of course it's possible to have great sex at home on the weekends, too. Many of us adore this relaxed time together. But not all of us. Spare a thought for the businessman or woman who can't spare much time off, or for the parents of young children – how do you ever get away from the little darlings? You can't. So my message is, if you can possibly afford it, set up temporary cover in the office or baby-care arrangements at home, and escape. *Every* couple should do this, on average every *six weeks*. After all, we're worth it.

Choosing a theme

If you want inspiration as to where to go
(should you be able to afford a break), that's
what this book is about. It's not possible
to mention specific resorts, but there are
suggestions to help you choose suitable sexual
terrain. Given that sex seems to have become
both a luxury and a recreation, I have come
up with ten very different themed weekends,
plus a stay-at-home scenario.

Each weekend is set in special surroundings,
such as in a **steamy hotel** in a throbbing city
like New Orleans, or in the pristine cold of a
ski resort. If you feel like exploring a little light
bondage, you might enjoy a hotel that has
fantasy rooms or, if you prefer your sex
to be "good old-fashioned dirty," then the
roadside motel is an obvious choice.

Each chapter contains ideas for equipment
you might need and love you might make!

What if you can't afford it?

The final chapter deals with this dilemma by
explaining that you might tell everyone that
you are going away, turn off all the phones,
pull down the blinds, and stay resolutely in
your own apartment – not giving the outside
world *another thought* until Sunday night.

Preparing for seduction

Your weekend surroundings will affect your feelings. If the hotel you choose turns out to be seedy and uncomfortable, you may become tense, or even feel disgust. Such sentiments do not encourage red-hot passion. So think beforehand about the kind of weekend you would like to explore and the *ideal place* in which to do it. If, for example, you love the idea of unleashing your darker side, pick a suitably gothic establishment or go for the brothel-style hotel room – they do exist.

Who should arrange the weekend?

Sound each other out to get a fair idea of what would be exciting. Try to do this *subtly*. For example, when you are making love one evening, you might say, "I've always wondered what it would be like to experience a bit of fun bondage. Have you ever thought about it? Do you have any strong feelings?"

Clearly, it's not a good idea to take a partner on an S&M weekend if you then discover that he or she is timid. The best rule is to take turns making the arrangements. Do this so that one of you cannot know what will happen. Part of the fun of a sexy weekend is *novelty,* and plenty of good sex is evoked by *anticipation and surprise*. So be prepared either to play the organizer or to let yourself be led.

Practice makes perfect

It can't hurt to fit in a bit of seduction practice before the planned weekend. Try taking turns being the active and the passive partner. Your task is to stimulate your lover with your hands and tongue so that he or she is **desperate** for sex. This will come in useful later because you will be familiar with his or her arousal pattern.

Prolonging your pleasure

Many sex games call for staying power, so if your man finds it hard to resist your magic hands, familiarize yourself with **the "squeeze" technique**. At the "point of no return," which you will learn to recognize or he will signal is near, squeeze the head of his penis hard between your finger and thumb, with the thumb just on or below the coronal ridge. This prevents ejaculation. Your next move is to stimulate your man's interest again. Practice on a pencil to get perfect.

Planning a scenario

If you have special interests, you may like to do a little extra advance planning. If, for example, you want to play a game where one of you is a police officer and the other is in trouble with the law, you might want to purchase a truncheon (there are some very suitable large vibrators), not to mention special uniforms. If you look forward to a sexual banquet, you'll want to visit the fruit and ice cream sections at the grocery store.

When you pack to go away, there are three **musts for the suitcase**: good quality lubricants; an inventive assortment of vibrators; and a trusty pack of condoms. If you are too busy or too timid to venture into a sex shop in reality, try doing so in virtuality. Good web addresses are: www.annsummers.com; www.condomania.com; www.passion8.co.uk; www.goodvibes.com; or www.thetoolshed.com.au.

Looking the part

Guys: we're talking about more than just the ordinary bath or shower routine here. Think about your appearance. Is your body attractive? Are there ways in which you might please or surprise your lover by changing something about it? For example, if you are very hairy, you might be curious to shave your body and discover what it feels like to be smooth. And not only women go for fake tans, men benefit from them, too.

Women: consider taking a leaf out of the younger generation's book. You might experiment with the surprise of letting your man discover you have a daring tattoo in a very private place. You don't have to go for a permanent tattoo, you can apply temporary transfers or use felt-tipped pen. If you have never styled your pubic hair, think about it. One woman I know dyed her pubes in overlapping shades of rose and pink.

Couples: part of the fun of all this relaxed time together is that you can lazily groom each other. From soaping and shampooing to hair and beard trimming, there are many grooming rituals that can be carried out alone – but are a lot more fun done together. Treat yourselves to a few luxury toiletries so that you will feel truly pampered.

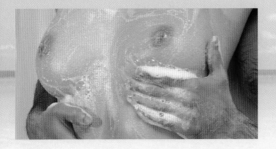

Anne J. Hooper

ANNE HOOPER

Relax and unwind

Summer in the Country

Green fields and trees, birdsong, and the dewy
freshness of the early morning – these all gladden
the heart. The countryside is the perfect place to
unwind, go for beautiful walks, and picnic in the
long grass. A country weekend gives you time
to *commune with nature* – and unashamedly
explore each other's bodies and sexual moods.

Creating the atmosphere...

True sensuality is preceded by *relaxed feelings*. It's important to pick the right venue with the right ambience because this will affect your mind and how you react sexually. Choose a country hotel where you can combine the pleasures of modern cuisine with the traditional delights of a four-poster bed and a roaring log fire, should the evenings grow cold.

Try to ensure that you are unlikely to meet anyone you know at the hotel – you should have *no inhibitions* whatsoever about breakfasting in bed, retiring to the bedroom in the afternoon, making the most of room service, or going to bed unusually early. Interruptions can also be passion-killers – so if you like to have a drink during lovemaking, make sure the beverage of your choice is already waiting for you in your room.

Pack your yoga mat: it might come in handy in the great outdoors.

Include a copy of the **Kama Sutra**: it contains some lovemaking positions that could be great for your countryside jaunt.

Take a picnic: offset the heaviness of the champagne bottle with dainty sandwiches and lightweight glasses.

Remember your walking shoes: you'll enjoy finding a quiet spot on a remote hillside where you won't be overlooked. It may be some distance away.

The Power of a Kiss

You are just back from your hike and glowing with the fresh air and exercise. This is an opportunity to gently *undress your lover*. Ease those shorts down his/her thighs. Slip the shirt up over his/her head. And kiss. Don't forget the power of the kiss ... it can be so wonderful that it reduces a lover to jelly and makes him/her desperate to get as close to you as possible. Perhaps you will have already succumbed to lips on lips during your country walk.

Sensational Touches

Extend your kissing to other parts of the body.
Kiss the toes, inside the arch of the foot, up the inside
leg as far as the thigh, then travel up to the breasts
and nipples. Combine your kissing at one end of her
body with finger stimulation at the other so that,
for example, your lover is turned on by your touch
along the inside of her armpits while you are
simultaneously kissing her thighs and genitals.
It creates a *double whammy* of sensation.

Exploring Erotic Spots

Some of the most erotic spots lie nowhere near the genitals. For example, the back of the neck, around the ears, and the ears themselves can be *so sensitive* that some individuals climax from ear stimulation alone. Always remember, everyone possesses different sensual zones, so what gives one person a fantastic climax might leave another cold. Feel free, therefore, to explore even the most innocent-seeming body sites. Don't worry if your roaming fingers do not provoke an instant reaction – this is just a *journey of discovery*.

The Art of Arousal

New moves need to be handled tactfully. One useful
rule is to do something new only when your partner is
virtually gasping for it. This is on the grounds that only
then will he or she be aroused enough for that next

move to be made. So if you are kissing your way around
his buttocks just *hint at* touching his anus before
actually doing so. If you are kissing her inner thighs,
wait until she positively arches her pelvis toward you.

Getting More Intimate

As your loving grows hotter, start working your way toward those most sensitive erogenous zones of all – the genitals. This is *mutual exploration*. But take your time even now. If you think he's desperate for you, explore his waist and kiss down along his abdomen. This can be an *acutely ticklish* area, but often ticklishness just adds to the experience. And don't forget the hidden zones – the right kind of touch on the back of the knee, for example, can drive a guy out of his mind.

Animal Passion

When finally you reach an explosive point of sensuality, through stroking and touching, this is a wonderful time to slip into *intercourse*. Maybe you'll want to try out some of the animal postures from the ***Kama Sutra*** (such as the "Crow" or "69" position, p.150), perhaps you need nothing except the here and now, the slip and slide of two feverish bodies. Revel in your human sexual instinct. By making love in the countryside you are truly at one with nature.

After the weekend...

Back in the hustle and bustle of normal life, remember the moment of *peace and contentment* after orgasm. In the best kind of lovemaking, lovers remain entwined, savoring the winding down of body and mind. Never instantly jump up and shower. Always rest, cuddle up together, and embrace each other as you slip into brief sleep. How you *behave after orgasm* makes a statement about your sensuality. Remember that ideally a wonderful sensual experience ends sensually as well.

Indulge in a little fantasy

Play Weekend

There's nothing like the new or the unknown to stimulate *erotic sensibility.* Staying in a friend's sumptuous loft apartment, for example, even in your own town, puts you in unfamilar surroundings. You will feel a little like strangers together…

Creating the atmosphere…

Having an entire apartment at your disposal means you can spread yourselves out and enjoy adopting someone else's *lifestyle* for a while. Perhaps that person has a different kind of love life. So if you have always wanted to pursue certain seductive pleasures, now might be the time to **step outside your own character** and into that of your "other self."

A little advance preparation could assist this personality transformation. So if you have an irresistible urge to smother each other in *ice cream* and then slowly and deliberately lick it off, visit the grocery store first. If erotic massage really appeals, then include feathers, silks, and satins in your suitcase.

The *scent* of your surroundings will deeply affect your mood – so if you want to feel sexy, you will be aided by sensual smells. Set the scene with some perfumed candles. Invest in sweet-smelling massage oils.

Ensure the apartment is *warm* and check the lighting. Glaring bright lights are stark and unflattering, whereas a soft, pinkish glow is cozy and complementary.

Exotic Ice Cream

With ice cream available in subtle new flavors like cardamom, mocha, and lavender, you'll enjoy taking your time over licking it off your partner's body. Choose your lover's most erotic spot and use it as a *plate*. Use the tongue like a palette knife, and with *broad sweeps* paint a provocative picture. If you lick the nipples, you'll know your technique is working when you see them swell upward and outward. The same is true of other key spots of the anatomy, too.

Role Play

The art of examining your patient is key to this game. Stay in role and insist that your patient **submits to your tests.** Explain that you need to check whether your patient is functioning properly and, in order to do this, he or she must

submit to your procedure. For her: check out her breast and clitoral response. For him: check out his testicles, penis, and anal response. If the patient objects, stress that this is necessary for the sake of their health.

Soft Strokes

Silk, velvet, and **peacock feathers** are the sensuous materials for an erotic massage. These luxurious substances glide across your nakedness, provoking tempting sensations. Skim the skin with these soft textures before moving on to use your hands. You might even blindfold your partner, and ask her to identify a variety of different materials. Only pay attention to the genitals after **petting and pampering** every other inch of the body first. A really good massage can be so arousing that genital sensation just blurs into a kind of overall heaven. All this without even reaching orgasm!

Mutual Masturbation

Goaded into a sensual frenzy by touching your lover's body, move on to mutual masturbation. With subtle fingers, pay serious attention to the genital area. ***Stroke, caress, and oil,*** just as you might the rest of the body. Build on your lover's responses and be unafraid to try firm strokes as well as fingertip caresses. Imagine that the vagina is a clock and try pressing the key "hours" on its rim. Treat the entrance to his anus in the same fashion.

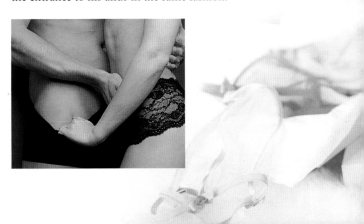

The Deer Exercise

According to Tao sexual instruction, the Deer Exercise facilitates semen production in men. You might ask your man to sit *cross-legged* and *flex* his anal muscles to build up control. A few men are capable of preventing ejaculation by clenching those perineal muscles so hard that they actually cut off the passage of semen. *Rubbing* the abdomen while cupping the genitals is said (by the ancient Chinese) to enhance the quality and quantity of semen. You might offer yourself as a *willing vessel* with whom your man can practice his self-control.

Slowing Down

The best sex is unhurried – *time is on your side*. The great thing about a weekend away is that you have two entire days removed from ordinary cares. This means that if you want to spend hours pleasuring each other's bodies with massage and foreplay, you can. There is absolutely *no compulsion* to hurry into orgasm. The build-up of this long-term loving often means that the whole body becomes wonderfully *sensualized*. Enjoyment is heightened – and when orgasm eventually happens, the experience is incredible.

After the weekend...

Every new experience changes us. A weekend in new surroundings is no exception, and a weekend devoted to sex often introduces you to an erotic "self" you may have dreamed about before but only now realize. You'll find that your mood has lifted. You feel more glamorous and adventurous. Your confidence has soared. Best of all, you feel attractive and sexy. In the future, you will be able to call on that *sexual self-belief.*

Turn up the heat

Winter Wonderland

Snow is *energizing*. You can bury yourself in a snowdrift and feel great. You can exhaust yourself on the ski slopes yet come home to a *lazy, sexy evening*. The icy touch of the white stuff draws us toward the warmth of a giant log fire and the intimacy of a candlelit evening. It's so romantic!

Creating the atmosphere...

It's cold outside and warm indoors and the very thought of *ice* next to the **naked skin** is **arousing**. So it's little surprise that this type of environment can promote some serious practicing of sexual technique.

It's worth remembering that for any form of sensuality to work well, be it massage or all-out sexual loving, the body needs to remain warm. This is because nerve endings in the skin constrict when affected by the cold and therefore touch is experienced as painful rather than pleasurable.

So make sure that your room stays *really cozy*. Crank up the stove and enjoy a steaming hot drink. Bear in mind that *glühwein* has long been considered the perfect après-ski reviver – and when you feel it warming you from the inside you'll begin to understand why.

The Warm-up

After a workout on the ski slopes, the first thing to do when you get home is to **collapse on to the sofa**. By the time you've enjoyed a warming drink and slumped against each other's shoulders, it's amazing how energy levels power up again. Don't be surprised if he starts pulling off your ski clothes. Don't be amazed when she starts caressing those trusty muscles – just to make you feel better, of course! This is the time for kisses and caresses.

In the Shower

The next move is to remove traces of the day's exertions that linger on the skin by taking a shower – *together*. All that soaping and rubbing puts you in a slithery kind of mood and the fact that the shower cubicle is really too small for two just adds to the excitement. It turns out to be vital that you *rub your body* against your lover's – it's the only way you can both fit into the tiny space. Well, that's the excuse anyway.

Pillow Fighting

Perhaps you start, halfheartedly, to get dressed
for your evening out and then one of you just
happens to cast your eye on those tempting, plump,
down-filled pillows. Oh dear. How could any feisty
lover resist? After the excitement and laughter of

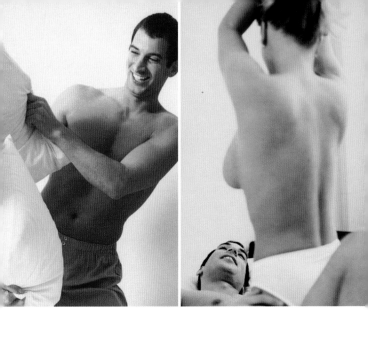

a pillow fight you simply fall on each other helplessly –
and then, somehow, you find that one thing leads to
another. Perhaps it's the *surprise of the attack* or
the playful blows of the pillow that have made you
feel sexy. But pillow fights are strangely arousing.

Sex on the Floor

The advantage of staying in a chalet rather than in a hotel is that you are in charge of your own environment. There's no one to complain when you **drag the mattress onto the floor** and lie together, bathed in heat yet aware that just outside the window is deep, deep snow. Just resting for a while in front of a crackling log fire eases muscle fatigue and allows latent sexual feelings to rise to the surface.

In Front of the Fire

Bathed only by the *flickering light of the fire*, it's easy to lose any inhibitions thanks to the semidarkness. The heat of the flames on your nakedness seems to draw out your sensuality. This is how your primeval ancestors

must have made love, back there in the cave. You feel primitive and that's how you act, swaying and bending, and shifting from position to position in a way you might not dream of in the bedroom back home.

After the weekend…

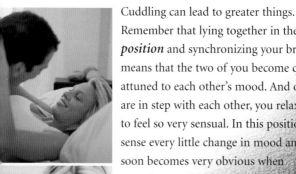

Cuddling can lead to greater things. Remember that lying together in the **spoons position** and synchronizing your breathing means that the two of you become quietly attuned to each other's mood. And once you are in step with each other, you relax and start to feel so very sensual. In this position, you sense every little change in mood and it soon becomes very obvious when one of you wants to take thing further. "Spoons" is also a marvelous starting point for lovemaking.

Feed your desire

Grand Passion

You want to stay glued together to the end. You are in the throes of a *tempestuous* love affair, and you are longing to devour one another. A weekend in a grand hotel is what you've been yearning for with all your heart.

Creating the atmosphere...

Your choice of hotel is important because it needs to be erotic. So think baroque, fantasy, or high-class brothel-style. Imagine the *florid grandeur* of the type of establishment you might find in an Anne Rice novel – a place that fuels the sexual imagination (not that it needs much of a trigger).

This is the *naughty* weekend – the one where perhaps you shouldn't even really be meeting one another but you are now so desperate for each other that absolutely nothing can stop you. This is the encounter where you might wear the wickedest of underwear and pack extra. That's because you'll need a spare after the first pair gets torn off the minute you step inside the hotel bedroom.

If this were one of the old capitals of Europe you would be arriving in a *fur coat* wearing only the very flimsiest brassière and panties underneath. Just walking through the hotel lobby gives you a buzz. If you've never tried it, you should. And when he lunges at you, attempting to shred the garments in his haste, don't be afraid to *tease* him a little – you hold back. That's assuming you are capable of restraining yourself in such a volcanic atmosphere.

Naked Desire

Clothes just get in the way. And yet ... *pulling, tugging,* and *lifting* garments from each other is all part of your intensity. Perhaps these efforts get hijacked by kissing each other so passionately that you can't stand up any longer – suddenly your legs give way. Perhaps you long to *submit* to one another, to *serve* and *seduce* so that the other has not the slightest chance of resisting. Sinking onto your bended knees, you longingly slide your lips down to your partner's genitals.

Steamy Bathing

Bathing, showering, and grooming become sensual aspects of seduction. Soaping each other all over, slowly combing the hair, even cutting the hair with sharp scissors, assume erotic proportions. Who would have thought that shampooing in warm water, with your lover's *slippery*

form *undulating* around yours, would be so hot? Who would have dreamed that you might send water cascading onto the floor as you slide helplessly into each other's bodies? It's hot, wet, and steamy in the bathroom and that's just how you feel inside – it's so passionate.

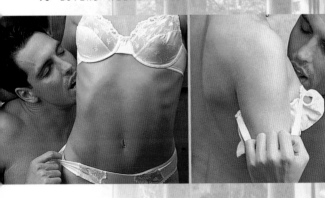

In the Hot Seat

Perhaps you decide to take a little break. A **snuggle together** on the grand chair brings you close, and maybe the two of you feel the flash of heat sparked by skin on skin. He shows a certain interest, she finds she can't help moving backward and forward across him. She shows a certain restlessness; he finds it so simple. All you have to do is to slip into that warm welcome and let yourself be **engulfed**. A little slow, lingering loving is in order.

Stockings and Garters

One of the great advantages of a high-passion weekend, away from everything that counts as everyday life, is the opportunity to **shed inhibitions** and act as you've never dared before. If you have always dreamed of being one of those erotic, arousing, purely **sexual beings**, now is the opportunity. If you have always wanted your partner to do or wear something a little different or unusual, this is the time. Stockings and garter belts are a saucy starting point.

Silks and Satins

The sexiest women know that their men get turned on by the *smoothness* of satin or a *wisp* of silk. Even the act of slipping these shiny fabrics over your naked body can arouse your guy. But tantalizing textures are not only alluring to men. For women, men's buttocks are more *sexually appealing* than any other part of the male anatomy, and viewing them clad in shiny silk briefs inspires a surprising amount of massage practice.

Taking the Lead

The sweetness of passion grows obvious when she crawls on top of his **naked body**, cradling his head, and kissing him passionately. There's something stimulating about even *thinking* about inching your way across your man, let alone doing it. And your guy is unlikely to object. Nearly every male will adore the idea of his woman taking the initiative. Especially when he knows she is motivated by unadulterated desire.

After the weekend...

When you live with intense sexual emotion, there are times when the experience becomes too much to contain. One of the outcomes of a passionate getaway together is that you often *relive key moments* over and over again during the following weeks, sometimes reaching, even in your lover's absence, further peaks of sexual desire. So how do you handle such desperate yearnings? The answer is to think about *pleasuring yourself* as your mind takes you, kiss by kiss, once more through that charged weekend.

Combine "crime" and passion

Murder Mystery

"Murder-mystery" weekends are often organized by hotels for guests who enjoy **playing the sleuth** and solving make-believe crimes. What the hosts don't know, and you do, is that the **skulduggery** of "murder" inspires some **exciting** bondage and seduction games in the privacy of your own room.

Creating the atmosphere...

Agatha Christie was almost as **daring** as some of the characters she invented for her crime novels. Perhaps, then, she would not have been too surprised by the possibilities offered by a classic murder weekend.

The ingredients you need are as follows: an **old-fashioned bed,** preferably with wooden bedposts; a few **silken ropes** and **ties**; a couple of **soft blindfolds**; a **mirror** in which you can watch your every move; plus optional access to a **grand piano**. This last is to be enjoyed sensually – rather than as the great composers originally intended.

Please take care not to do anything that will offend other guests in the party. However inspirational a murder weekend might be to you, it is not intended to be a sex orgy, and the other participants might justifiably object. This means, in practice, that your personal detecting should take place in the *privacy of your bedroom*, with the doors locked and room service on hold. Getting into the private side of a murder suspect's character, however, as you struggle while tied "brutally" to the bed, may lead to some *inspired sleuthing*.

Tying up Your Victim

How does it feel to be **trussed up** and **helpless**, like a "murder victim"? Help your lover find out by telling him that he will be given a very sexy time indeed, provided that he agrees to have his hands **tied** behind him and that he submits to a **blindfold**. Not being able to see will increase the acuteness of his other senses. Test your "victim's" sensory reflexes by caressing certain parts of his anatomy. How you conduct the test is up to you. All he needs to know is that he must pass it. Or else!

Piano Duet

When you are **certain** that the
other guests are safely absent, sneak
into the music room and practice a
few scales on the piano. Remember
the movie, *Pretty Woman,* and that
passionate scene on top of the grand
played by Richard Gere and Julia
Roberts? Well, here's your chance to
copycat. But there's a twist: as you
lean menacingly across your lover,
plant the **suggestion** in his/her
head that he/she just might become
the "murderer's" next casualty.

Hidden Pleasures

Have you ever played the game of *sardines*? That's the one where lots of you cram into a tiny space and hide, without moving or saying a word. The last one to find the group is the loser – and in more ways than one. He's missed out on those breathless, overheated moments of being squashed by and squeezed against the bodies of his friends. Now is your chance to "hide from the murderer." Make the most of it.

She who disobeys…

The "job" of the **dominator** is to find fault with the victim, however perfectly she obeys. This means fining her for misdemeanors she didn't even know she was committing. How to punish? You might: stroke her where she's ticklish; spank

her on the backside enough to sting but not so
hard as to hurt; or caress her between the legs and
take your hand away just as it's getting interesting.
Much of the stimulation comes in *waiting for the
punishment*, rather than from the act itself.

Sofa Antics

The dominator might ***demand*** that his victim pleasures him exactly as he wishes. This does not guarantee that he gets entirely what he wants, of course, because she may anticipate interesting punishments and deviate from his instructions. But she will also want to pleasure him, so she may beat him at his own game. If she is giving him ***oral sex***, for example, as he sits on the sofa, she might take him to a ***fever pitch of excitement*** and then refuse absolutely to go any further!

Playing "dead"

One very apt challenge for a murder weekend is to see how long you can lie absolutely still while your partner *caresses you all over*. Take turns being the *"corpse."* It's surprisingly difficult to remain motionless if you are being stimulated so expertly that you are not only becoming seriously aroused, but are also in serious need of a climax. When it's the man's turn, he is allowed his erection, but *no* other type of movement.

After the weekend…

If only one of you has experienced being blindfolded and then submitted to sexual "torture," the other might like to try this out when you get back to real life and real time. It's worth **agreeing** in advance on a **code word** that you can use if you really want the action to cease. This means you can scream out desperately, "Stop, stop" without really meaning it. But the code word is an **absolute signal**.

Feel the rhythm

Dancefloor Drama

There's something about performing the tango, strutting the rumba, or holding each other tight to the strains of Cuban rhythms that gets the *heart racing*. Just a few simple steps to the throb of dance music is enough to launch you into a weekend of movement and *passionate sex*.

Creating the atmosphere...

The sight of a talented couple performing the *tango* is so arousing it's enough to make grown men and women fall on each other in a frenzy of lust. The hallmark sensual, gyrating movements of this erotic dance compare to a kind of *visual foreplay*. Small wonder that exotic dancing appeals to couples intent on sparking deep passion within their lives. Is it the sound of the melodic beat? Or the vision of long, loose limbs encircling other slim bodies? Or is it the *simulation* of sexual intercourse you see before you on the dance floor that gets you so hot?

Latin American dance classes and workshops are held in dance studios all around the world. Opt for a workshop in an exotic city and do a little homework to find yourselves a hacienda-style hotel, preferably close to the dance premises. In between your dance classes and lovemaking, feast your palate on some memorable Latin American cuisine. If you adore movement and rhythm, surround yourself with wonderful music in your hotel room and don't be afraid to practice. Above all, ***don't forget the rose*** – you'll need it to grasp between your teeth!

Flirting

There's something about Latin music that brings you alive. It's so upbeat that it makes you feel *happy* and *flirtatious*, even if you were miserable beforehand. Laughing and joking together can start some of the best sex. So think of your first day of dancing as a wonderful way to enliven your mood. Abandon yourselves to the *sensuality* of the music. Have fun, laugh, hug, and snuggle. This flirtatious behavior will put you in a sexier, more relaxed frame of mind.

Nonstop Tango

The tango must be the hottest dance ever invented. Small wonder that, having turned each other on during the practice session, you simply have to continue your performance in the bedroom. You might rehearse your steps naked in your suite or hotel room. As you slither around each other and let the music throb through your very being, you may grow so *inflamed with desire* that you cannot resist sliding out of your dance position and into some truly hot sex.

Slow Waltz

The waltz contains a *suggestive* and *sensual* pattern of steps. When the dance was first introduced, decent young women were forbidden to perform it for fear that they would be corrupted. As you hold each other close, feel your partner's every moment by pressing *intimately* against his or her thighs and pelvis. The closer you move, the more opportunity you have to kiss and nuzzle your lover's neck and face. It's very easy to get lost as you glide along in such intimate proximity.

Alfresco Interval

Physical exercise, such as dancing, relaxes couples and helps them feel comfortable and trusting. The intimacy of dancing might lead most satisfactorily to different kinds of sensual moves – those involving your mouths. Try the delicious experiment of sipping wine from each other's belly buttons. Or nibble on an olive together. The best extra-virgin olive oil has more uses than you might think … *licking, sucking,* and *rubbing* it into tender skin can be delicious! Just make sure that no one else can see you when you decide to assuage your appetite.

Stairway to Heaven

When you return, hot and sticky, from your dance class, don't head straight for the shower. Put the heat you have generated to work by launching into an alternative type of exercise. Perhaps you will be so eager that you won't somehow quite make the bedroom but collapse with desire on the stairs. There are times when the sensation of cold marble against hot skin makes you want to get as ***close as humanly possible***. And if he needs a little inspiration, try stroking him gently with a beautiful red rose.

Grand Finale

As you become more in step, anticipating each other's every movement, the greater is your capability to become more mentally attuned. Some people achieve a kind of *emotional ecstasy* through a blend of dance and sex. They feel so enriched by their dancing that they are already close to nirvana. The experience of quiet lovemaking, where you lie close or nibble your lover's neck, can be enough to prolong the sensual mood begun earlier during the dance.

After the weekend...

Dancing is good exercise, so when you return home, don't be tempted to become immobile again – try to keep physically active. Immobility leads to stiffness. And stiff individuals don't become terribly passionate. There's a real link between *body flexibility* and *great lovemaking*. So get up, stroll around, flex your arms and legs and, if you are lucky enough to be at home with your partner, sweep him or her into a *tantalizing* tango.

Gourmet Hideaway

Renting or borrowing an out-of-the-way apartment for the weekend means you can be assured of complete *privacy* – and a kitchen. Should you be serious "foodies," you'll adore the idea of *putting each other on the menu*.

Creating the atmosphere...

Think about the provisions you might need for your gourmet weekend. Fruit is ideal for tempting "picnics" because it can be prepared to look exotic. A platter of grapes, pear slices, jewel-like raspberries, split bananas, and luscious strawberries is an erotic sight in itself.

You might have a taste for the *lovers' banquet*, where you decorate each other with delectable fruit, cream, and honey, and then lick your way through the spread.

In addition to this sensual feast, make time for a long bath – together – in which you drink *long flutes of champagne* and dribble it down each other's bodies. All this is the perfect preliminary to some gourmet lovemaking later.

Don't be afraid to make these arrangements beforehand. There is nothing wrong with a little forward planning. There are *tantalizing* pleasures to be had from *anticipating* a sensual getaway … long before you've even left town.

In the Kitchen

Perhaps you love the turn-on of coming across your partner, in the *nude*, doing the *housework*. Maybe you want to see his/her naked body sitting up on the *counter* where you prepare the evening meal – it's the contrast of ideas that gives you a real jolt. Or is it the anticipation of a little food and a little sex that makes your mouth water? Or perhaps your naked meeting in the kitchen just gives you a *tender moment*?

Raiding the Icebox

Equip yourself with an *ice cube* and a *hot drink*. First, rub the ice cube around your lover's nipple. Take a gulp of steaming liquid, and then encircle the nipple in your hot mouth. The stark contrast of hot and cold sensation is incredible and affects not only the breasts but most of the body. Alternatively, ice your mouth first, rather than applying ice directly to the body.

Sensual Massage

You don't need the full-body experience to get fabulous erotic sensation from a massage. A head, neck, or facial massage can produce exquisite *prickles of delight* that flood the entire torso. The head is also a good place to start if you want to ease your partner into a relaxed, sensual mood. After gently massaging the scalp, you can go on to more *daring strokes*, such as rubbing the shoulders, the abdomen … and eventually the genitals.

Turning up the Heat

Moving on to *cunnilingus* right after a massage feels like a natural progression. Having stimulated the whole body with your hands, now you want to get more specific. Perhaps she is in a hurry to get to the bedroom and you have waylaid her by giving her such unexpected *oral pleasure* that she has stopped right there in front of you. You have a very good idea that in a minute she might slip to the floor and beg for more. You might use your hands to hold her open as you *lick upward*.

Anal Massage

Over the weekend, you want to introduce each other
to new sensation. If you've never tried it, anal massage
could be the novel activity. The anus has no natural
lubricant of its own so, using a well-lubricated finger,
begin to **probe the outer rim** of her anal passage.
This is full of **nerve endings** and simply by stretching
the rim you offer a sensation-laden starting point. The
wider she is stretched, the nearer you get to being able
to slip inside for anal intercourse.

Putting on a Show

If he is very visually responsive, you may know what effect you have when you *strip slowly* and *sensuously* in front of him. Find an area that you can use for pretend pole-dancing, lift your legs up high, curve,

and turn. Slowly disrobe as you move and sway, then
offer him a bottle of massage oil. Ask him to rub it all
down your gleaming body, as you stand naked in
front of him. Only do this if you know he'll love it.

After the weekend…

Relaxed weekends are a reminder that loving touch is good for us. It calms and soothes us and lifts our spirits. And just as it helps to lighten our mood, it follows on that it makes us feel sensual, too. ***Don't forget the power of a hug, an embrace, or a quiet snuggle.*** Your partner's loving touch has the power to relieve depression, restore your self-confidence, and make you feel good about yourself once more.

Experience sexual ecstasy

Spiritual Retreat

Tantric sex allows us to gain **balance** in life. Should you manage to attain **ecstasy** through Tantric sex, this is considered the part of a life force that lets you become a "higher" human being. A **Tantric sex weekend** introduces you to a different way of experiencing sex.

Creating the atmosphere...

An important part of Tantric sex is to "feel" what your partner is feeling when you touch and stroke him/her. The longer you caress, the more *in tune* you become with their thoughts as well as your own. Imperceptibly, your sensuality becomes *merged* with theirs. You become "as one." In order to achieve this state of union, your time needs to be unhurried. A long weekend, away from people and telephones, is the perfect opportunity.

At the beginning of your weekend, take long walks and get plenty of sleep. You need to be completely relaxed for the Tantric sex exercises so that you can attempt to contain your orgasm. Unlike the Western practice of climaxing fast, Tantra **draws out** the process, believing that there is greater spirituality in keeping yourself on the edge for long minutes, even hours. If you can cast your mind back to blissful occasions of **extreme arousal** when you were almost climaxing, you can see that the ancient priests had a point. Tantra also teaches a process to prolong climax.

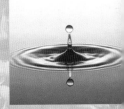

The Tantric Kiss

The wonderful aspect of the Tantric kiss is that it is far more than simply an adjunct to the important business of sex. Kissing is valued as a ***peak erotic experience*** in its own right. Sensitive kissing can set the body on fire and feel so incredible that some women even climax from it. So don't be in a hurry to move on from the meeting of the lips. Savor the experience and let it happen again and again.

Merging Orgasmic Emotion

Sit across from each other in a warm room, and take turns slowly stroking each other all over. Use massage oil to make your hands slippery. As you stroke, instead of feeling the sensation your hand is receiving, *tune into the sensation* his skin is getting from you. On the second and third occasion, make this more sexual and don't be afraid of stroking to the point of orgasm – using the squeeze technique (squeezing the penis hard between finger and thumb) to prevent ejaculation.

Exchanging the Vital Force

Ancient Tantric belief has it that a mixture of love juices, or the secretions of mouth and vagina, creates an *exchange of life force*. This is because when sexual juices are absorbed by the mouth during mutual stimulation, the masculine and feminine energies, or *yin* and *yang,* combine to form a whole. The "69" position, known as "the Crow" in Tantric manuals, is thought to create "a natural circuit of psychic energy."

Union of the Soul

The Tantric sitting position has the man sitting cross-legged while his partner sits between his legs with her own wrapped around his waist. As you cradle each other closely, you rise and fall just enough to maintain his sexual interest. In this slow fashion, you can prolong intercourse until you feel the need for climax so strongly you can no longer wait. The act of orgasm is believed to allow lovers to "dissolve" into each other's *individual souls*.

The Tantric Athlete

Tantric erotic poses were designed to create *equilibrium* in body and spirit. Why do we need sexual balance? The ancients believed that it led to self-realization, perhaps because we can only reach a peak when we no longer struggle with difficulty. A common pose in erotic Hindu art is the intertwined "Sexual athlete", where the woman perches halfway up her standing man, supported by his arms. Only try this if you possess great strength.

Taking Your Time

Because men are usually stronger than their female partners, they are considered, where Tantra is concerned, to have a special responsibility. When he enters her from above, he is able to savor his sense of power and strength. Yet precisely because of this, he is also exhorted to **remain sensitive** to his woman's needs. The man-on-top position (which affords deep penetration) offers far better sensation when intercourse is deliberately unhurried and drawn out. So practice the principle of taking your time.

After the weekend…

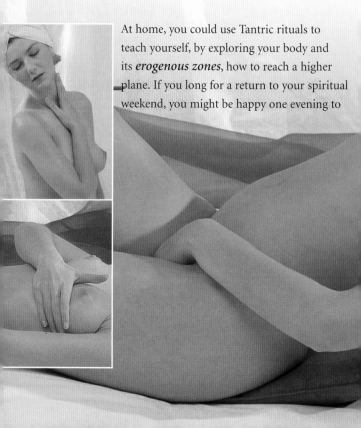

At home, you could use Tantric rituals to teach yourself, by exploring your body and its *erogenous zones*, how to reach a higher plane. If you long for a return to your spiritual weekend, you might be happy one evening to

caress your own body and sex organs.
Through touch and deep breathing, *open up*
your sexual response as far as you can. You are
working toward a Tantric wholeness.

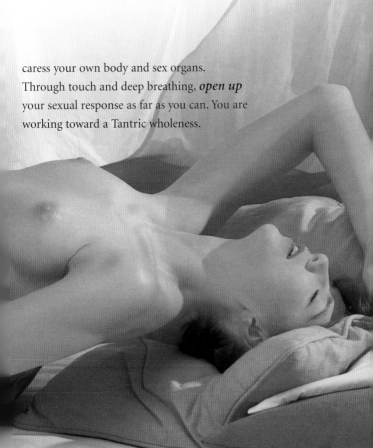

Will you obey orders?

Bondage
Escapade

You've longed to experience the **pleasure and pain** of being rendered helpless. And now you've met a partner whose desire dovetails perfectly with yours. It is with heightened anticipation (and some trepidation) that you prepare to succumb to your partner's **power**.

Creating the atmosphere...

To get the most from your weekend, you'll want to put some thought into choosing your bondage garments. These are not clothes for everyday use, but wet-look plastics and rubber, designed to be *ultra-tight* and *ultra-tempting*.

To accompany these you might wish to purchase a soft rubber flail, a pair of soft handcuffs, and a variety of whips, ties, and harnesses. If he is dying for you to treat him like the *ultimate doormat*, steeple-high heels are a must.

But when you slip on the slinky outfits, you also need to don a new *attitude* toward sex. Should you be the dominant partner, you need

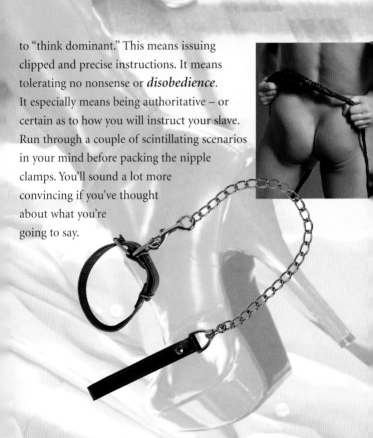

to "think dominant." This means issuing clipped and precise instructions. It means tolerating no nonsense or *disobedience*. It especially means being authoritative – or certain as to how you will instruct your slave. Run through a couple of scintillating scenarios in your mind before packing the nipple clamps. You'll sound a lot more convincing if you've thought about what you're going to say.

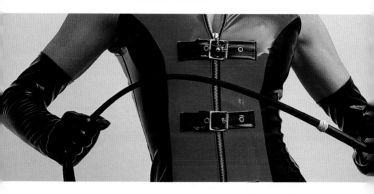

Dressing the Part

Faced with a ***gleaming, rubber-clad*** woman, a number of powerful emotions flit through the male mind – apprehension, admiration, sneaking desire, and sheer nervousness. Glistening, high-heeled boots and a matching whip complete the outfit, but the pose only works if you hold yourself erect and make it clear that your partner is merely a worm who crawls upon the earth. Dressing the part definitely helps you to get into character and encourages him to believe that ***you are the one in charge.***

Means of Punishment

Use **only** paddles, whisks, or soft flails for punishment – they arouse the flesh pleasantly but don't hurt. You might order your partner to keep still and when you discover he has moved (a fraction), reprimand him. Alternatively, you might ask your partner where he would like to be punished. And when he tells you, **direct your strokes** to a site other than the preferred one. The idea is to take your lover by surprise with your actions.

Slave Labor

Your slave is expected to carry out your **slightest whim**, be it to lick the ground clean in front of you, or to pleasure you with his/her tongue. You might use a harness or cord to strap up your partner in a provocative manner, winding the material in and around the genitals and (if female) around the breasts. As a kind of payoff you might **stimulate your lover** in any manner you choose, telling him/her that he/she must submit to whatever you do.

High Heels

Some men (and a few women, too) are shoe fetishists. The best shoes for sex are those with ultra-high heels, preferably made from toughened perspex, that look as if they would create serious damage should you walk all over your man in them. The trick is to **threaten to step on him**, to press the shoe in sinister fashion into the flesh, but **not** actually to put your full weight on them. It is the idea, or impression, of cruelty that you want to give, rather than the actual experience.

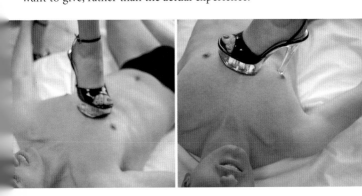

Breast Worship

Winding straps around your woman's full breasts,
or squeezing them into rubber garments and then
fondling them while they are trussed up, satisfies
the *deepest fantasies* of many men and some
women. You might try breast massage during these
explorations, where you not only stimulate the full
breast, but also stroke down the sides of the breast,
sliding your fingertips across the breast like a spider,
and ending by closing your fingers on the nipple and
drawing them away. Try gently *rubbing her nipples*
while moving in and out of her during intercourse.

Taking Control

If you have been playing the dominatrix, the time will come when you want to **ride your man** in order to obtain your supreme pleasure. He will understand that he has to fall in with your commands and do everything that you ask. This is not for him, you tell him, as you work toward your own pleasure. He is merely a **willing vessel** – he exists only to serve you. Maybe afterward you will reward him, but don't tell him that right now.

After the weekend...

Building on the success of your bondage weekend, use some of the actions and techniques that really worked for the two of you. If anal sex was what turned you on, then don't be afraid of ***being really suggestive*** the next time you are relaxed together in the bedroom. If using vibrators is what did it, then invest in several different models, bearing in mind there are many now for men as well as women.

Will you get caught?

Sex in the City

There are many thwarted *exhibitionists* – men and women – among us, who long to explore sex in *public places* but who do not do so because it might cause offense. One way of meeting this need is to play out *special sex scenarios* so that (in your mind) you feel transported to *forbidden territory*.

Creating the atmosphere...

You might love the idea of having sex in a
public place where you risk being caught. But
since you will not want to break any laws, you
will appreciate the value of **acting out** fantasies
or scenarios as an alternative.

The next best thing to having sex in the
public library, or in the office after dark, is
to play at it. In practice, this involves **setting
up** certain situations to lend a real edge to
your activities.

If your partner adores the idea of **sex in the office**, arrange to take him to a friend's apartment where one of the rooms has been converted into an office.

If love among the book stacks is your idea of heaven, explore the possibility of borrowing a **librarian's key** so that you can use the premises after dark.

Meeting as **"strangers"** in a real bar, with her pretending to be the working girl and him acting as the john, is surprisingly arousing. And when she takes him "home," it could be to a friend's place where the bedroom has been exotically decorated for the night and where he had absolutely no idea he would be led. It is this element of the unexpected that provides the important sexual "frisson."

Provocative "Strangers"

Him: as a "stranger," stand close to your lover on a crowded train. You might slide your hand down the back of her skirt (provided it cannot be seen) and stroke underneath it. Watch her face while you do so.

Her: make a point of picking up something from the floor in front of him. If you are wearing a short skirt and high heels, the act of bending will pull the skirt up at the back. Are you wearing anything underneath?

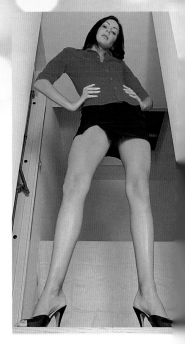

Sex Between the Bookshelves

Strictly after closing time, **visit the library** for a little extracurricular study. On this occasion, she might pleasure him, paying close attention to his penis. To be particularly provocative, he might read while urging her on to greater efforts. Using her **tongue as a guitar pick,** she might strum it across his penis, letting it catch and pull along the frenulum (on the underside of the head of the penis) and the coronal ridge. Hopefully, he will find it so hard to concentrate that he drops his book.

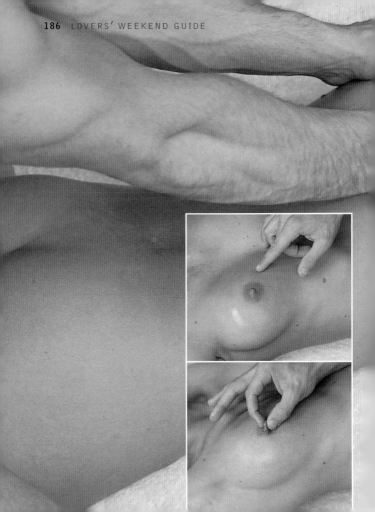

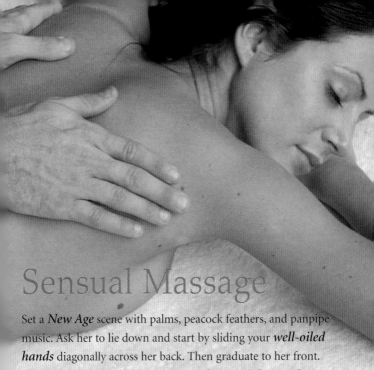

Sensual Massage

Set a **New Age** scene with palms, peacock feathers, and panpipe music. Ask her to lie down and start by sliding your **well-oiled hands** diagonally across her back. Then graduate to her front. Make spirals on her breasts with your fingers. Slide your finger and thumb toward each other across the breast, meeting up and lifting off over the nipple. Then **blindfold** her, tell her your colleague must now practice his massage strokes on her, and leave the room. When you return, pretend to be the colleague.

Hell's Angels

There's a *surprise* for your man. You have had your *nipples pierced*. (If you don't want the real thing it is possible to fake it.) Explain that you have undergone this rite to demonstrate how devoted you are to him,

the leader of the Hell's Angels. Now explain that you will let him tattoo your body with any motif he likes and offer him a blue marker (indelible pencil works also well here). Then tell him, very quietly, that you will submit to any kind of sex he desires.

Playing Boss and Secretary

It's late and the staff has left **the office**. The lights are low and the computer is turned off. "Miss Jones," he instructs, "take off your clothes." Then "Sit, Miss Jones and spread your legs." As you wait obediently with sharpened pencil in hand, he gives you dictation in the form of **tongue on clitoris**. "Miss Jones," he tells you, halfway through, "you are absolutely forbidden to cry out." You are forced to experience a silent orgasm. Such hardship!

Sex in the Elevator

This game is only to be performed in the middle of the night at a friend's home where there is an elevator. Even though you have set this up to be totally private, tell your lover that you might be *interrupted* at any moment. Yet insist that you get it on either in the elevator or outside it. To add to the *flow of adrenaline*, press the call button a couple of times so that the elevator travels between floors. It's scary yet safe.

After the weekend...

For any game to work well, it must have an aspect of *novelty*. And back home, there's no reason why new activities cannot still be introduced from time to time. If you haven't yet used one together, a vibrator is an excellent toy to play with. There are *ring-shaped vibes* that fit around the base of his penis, giving pleasure to you both during intercourse, and *double vibrators* and cute *finger vibrators* that you can use to take each other by surprise under the table at dinner parties!

Explore your wild side

Motel Lust

Unashamed, pure sex is one very good reason for spending the weekend with your lover. The seediness of the roadside motel adds strangely to your pleasure. It encourages you to **liberate** yourself and be more **extrovertly sexual** than perhaps you could be in normal surroundings.

Creating the atmosphere...

Since this is going to be a strictly clothes-off, no-holds-barred weekend, you won't have to stock up on any special equipment. But since you will be spending the majority of your time *naked*, you might take special care beforehand to make sure your body looks as *attractive* as possible. And yes, this does apply to men, too!

If you are male you might, as an experiment, try shaving your body so that a *gleaming*, *hairless* individual sweeps his partner off her feet. Don't forget to treat yourself to a self-massage using a good quality oil. To be really imaginative, try spraying yourself with stardust or body gleamer. Take a look around your pharmacy for such products or research them online.

If you are female you might like to go for an *all-over tanning* treatment and some interesting depilation around the pubic area.

Face to Face

You may feel compelled to kiss for as long and as
often as possible. Perhaps you **can't physically keep
your faces apart** – you're virtually drinking from
each other's mouths as you press your bodies tight.
All thoughts of your motel surroundings have
vanished, disappearing into a world of sensation.
Yet even while you breathe into each other's mouths,
experiencing moments of great tenderness, you ache
with arousal and desire.

Armchair Passion

Perhaps you were sitting quietly in a ***comfortable chair*** in the dark, getting your breath back, when sheer lust somehow started things up again. Maybe he nuzzles you, perhaps you press just that bit closer to him, but before you know it, he's driving you to ***distraction*** with all that nuzzling and licking. Quite soon you slide on top of his erection and find yourself opening up completely to ***passion***, leaning all the way back and letting him do anything he (and you) wants.

Across the Armchair

Seeing that she has **raised her buttocks** from the side of an armchair especially for you to penetrate her from the rear has a profound effect on you. It gives you the idea that you can indulge all your lustful thoughts without, for once, concentrating on hers. Don't forget that many women need *additional stimulation* on the clitoris to get any real sensation this way. Yet just the fact that she is doing this to please only you can electrify the atmosphere.

Raunchy Behavior

Not for you the straightforward sex of the missionary position. You are eager to experience sensuality in every possible pose. *Lovemaking on a chair* allows him to achieve the maximum thrust needed during a rear-entry position or while standing up. And in your eagerness to *experiment* with every sex position in the book, you even have a shot at the wheelbarrow (below right). This latter is for fun since it won't offer tons of stimulation, but it does enable you to feel youthfully athletic.

The White Tiger

The ancient Chinese illustrated the sex-from-the-rear position, calling it the White Tiger, in their pillow-books. The incredibly rare tiger presumably leapt on its mate with the kind of *passion* equated with savagery. When sex from the rear is experienced as hard and as blatantly as it is here, you can see why the pose is likened to the beautiful but savage beast. Even the word "white" evokes the impression of *white-hot passion*. Whipping her clitoris into a matching rhythm is part of this mating frenzy.

Sixty-nine

Many lovers consider the 69 position to be one of ultimate intimacy. Each lover is opened to the other in *supreme proximity*, tasting and scenting the other's body. As each partner is provoked into near climax, he/she returns the favor *simultaneously*.

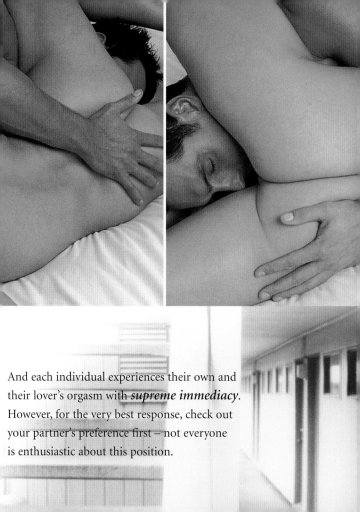

And each individual experiences their own and their lover's orgasm with **supreme immediacy**. However, for the very best response, check out your partner's preference first – not everyone is enthusiastic about this position.

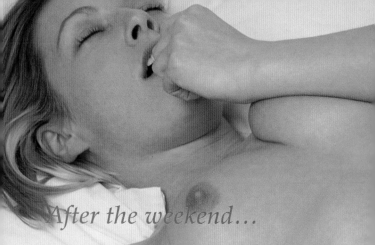

After the weekend…

Eager to remember the closeness you achieved on your motel weekend, you might want to revisit some of those intimate moments.
Sex in a room other than the bedroom is just one possibility. But if you are unable to obtain privacy, don't forget the thrill of *incredible oral sex*. Treat each other to fellatio and cunnilingus exclusively. Take turns so that each of you feels the other's attention and concentration being single-mindedly focused on you alone.

Make the most of time alone

Home Alone

There are occasions when you long for
quality time together, but cannot afford to
stay away from home. Yet you are desperate
to leave the interruptions and free your mind
for wonderful *erotic encounters* only.
Here's how you manage it.

Creating the atmosphere...

Tell friends and family that you are going away for the weekend and will be out of contact. Then *pull down the blinds* and hole up for the next two days. Silence the telephone and switch on the answering machine or activate your message service. If either of you work from an office at home, lock the door and hide the key in a safe place.

The refrigerator should be amply stocked, ideally with the most tempting, exotic foods you can think of. Go for treats you wouldn't usually snack on.

Vow to each other that this weekend is devoted wholly to *sexual experimentation* and to satisfying your curiosity. Everything you do, even if it is reading a book, will be with a view to widening your erotic horizons. And contemplate, beforehand, what avenues these might be. For example, if you've always longed to include *moviemaking* in your erotic repertoire, make sure the camera is nearby. If the idea of playing doctor and nurse gets you going, don't forget to give some thought to the medical uniform you might wear.

Film Fun

Your goal is to end up with the *sexiest movie possible* – one that you can replay over and over again. So if stripping slowly and seductively gets you going, the removal of her panties or his briefs must be done slowly and sensuously. You can *zoom in* on your partner's buttocks as well as pulling back to catch his or her face. Have fun catching your partner doing an erotic Pilates exercise or shoot dirty by angling upward at her crotch. Alternatively, spread a few Polaroids around.

Different Rooms

By shutting yourself away at home for the weekend you can be assured of absolute privacy in rooms other than the bedroom. For example, you might be *in the kitchen*, ironing out creases in your policewoman's outfit, when your partner sidles in. You realize that he can't wait for you to put the uniform on. Be careful. Don't burn yourself! Or perhaps it's never occurred to you to seduce your partner in your *bathroom*. Now's your chance to take him by surprise …

Sex Books

If you've ever longed to try out some of those exotic poses you read about in sex manuals, now is the perfect opportunity. Take turns choosing an unusual sex position (even if it is one that looks ridiculous!) and agree that each will humor the other. *No cheating here*. If she turns out to be reading a cookbook while you are busy doing your homework, give her a suitably devised punishment. She'll probably love it.

Net Encounters

Ever heard of virtual swinging? This is when you
don't actually meet other couples in person but
you get to know them, their turn of phrase, and
their *favorite sexual activities*, online, via your
computer. Make this a joint activity so that you
write your erotic messages together, and, while
waiting for the other couple's reply, put into *practice*
some of the ideas you have just been describing over
the internet. It will give you further inspiration!

Sexual Bonding

You don't have to be a fetishist to think that men and women look desirable when bound in *shiny tape*. It can be used to exaggerate sexual features, such as the breasts, or to bind the arms behind the back or to the sides of the body, rendering your lover helpless. A great new variation is to acquire some bondage wrap. This deep-colored cling wrap comes in rich shades of black, scarlet, and brilliant pink, and makes a lover look extraordinary.

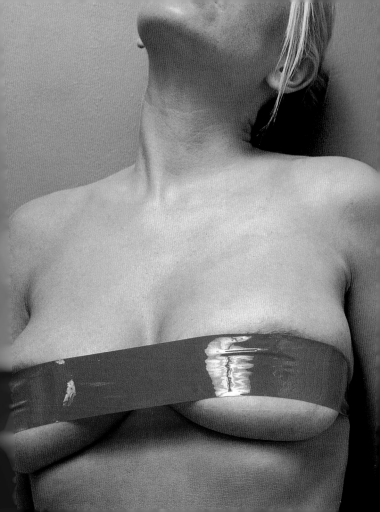

Strip to Tease

You happen to know that he adores you looking
lewd *and nude*. And it's one of those strange
truths that undressed women look best when
wearing a few strategically placed items of clothing.
It's also a fact that men are turned on by what they

see and that many of them can get ready
for action simply by homing in on a lover's
incredibly long legs topped by strappy garters.
So here's to do the *slow and subtle* striptease.
And its outrageous effect!

After the weekend…

Washing, shampooing, brushing the hair, shaving the beard – these can all send erotic shivers up the spine when someone else does them for you. So if your partner has indulged you on your stay-at-home weekend, remember how wonderful this felt and try, occasionally, to **build a little mutual care into everyday life**. Thinking back to how your lover's touch sparked those prickles of desire should render this none too difficult!

Enjoying Safer Sex

By practicing safer sex, you can help to
protect yourself against HIV (human-
immuno-deficiency virus, AIDS (acquired
immune deficiency syndrome), and other
sexually transmitted infections (STIs) such
as genital warts, herpes, gonorrhoea, syphilis,
and chlamydia.

What is safer sex?

Safer sex is any kind of sexual activity that
does not involve the **exchange of bodily
fluids**. When the penis penetrates the vagina
during unprotected intercourse, the woman is
exposed to the man's semen and he is exposed
to her vaginal fluids. Since viruses and other
infections may be transmitted in these fluids,
this is a potentially risky activity. However,
if either the man or woman wear a condom,
then neither partner is exposed to the other's
fluids and risk is significantly reduced.

Is oral sex safe?

Oral sex also *carries a risk* because semen
and vaginal fluids come into contact with the
mucous membranes of the mouth. If these
membranes are broken or ulcerated in some
way (by cold sores or bleeding gums, for
example), HIV can enter the body via infected
semen or vaginal fluid. You can make oral sex
safer by using a condom during fellatio and
a latex barrier during cunnilingus.

Who should practice safer sex?

Anyone who has concerns or doubts about the
sexual health or history of a sexual partner
should practice safer sex.

Only if you *both* have a *clean bill of health*
and you have sex only with each other is it safe
to avoid practicing safer sex.

Using Condoms

When it comes to protection against HIV, condoms are the safest form of contraception. There are many different types and brands: colored, flavored, textured, and even some with special attachments. As long as the packet bears a recognized mark and a use-by date, you can be free to be experimental. Buy a selection of unusual condoms and try them, giving each condom a rating.

Keep them handy

You don't want to have to stop and search for a condom at the critical moment – keep one under your pillow so that you can just slip it out when needed. Hide condoms in secret places around the house so that you can enjoy impromptu sex wherever you are.

Smooth application

Teach yourself how to put condoms on slowly and quickly, in the dark, using only one hand.

Practice makes perfect, and if you want to hone your skills on a dummy penis, try a cucumber. Put a condom on your partner as you stimulate his penis with your hands and tongue. You could also try slipping the condom into your mouth so that you put it on him as you bear down during oral sex.

Games

- Experiment with different methods for putting on condoms, depending on their color or flavor.
- Time your partner's speed at putting the condom on your penis.
- Tell her that she has got to break the world record in slipping a condom on so unobtrusively that you do not notice.

Index

A

B

C D

Acknowledgments

Photography: **Luke Beziat, Peter Pugh-Cook, James Muldowney**

Picture researcher: **Anna Bedewell**
Picture librarian: **Romaine Werblow**

The publisher would like to thank the following for their kind permission to reproduce their photographs: (Abbreviations key: t=top, b=bottom, r=right, l=left, c=centre. GI = Getty Images, EWA = Elizabeth Whiting & Associates, NT = National Trust Photographic Library) **6-7, 8-9:** GI: Chris Huxley; **8:** Masterfile UK: Zoran Milich (cl); **9:** NT: Alasdiar Ogilvie (cr); **11:** GI: Chris Huxley, EWA (b); **12:** GI: Angela Wyant (cl); **12-3:** GI: Chris Huxley; **14:** Corbis: Craig Tuttle (tl), **14-5, 16-7:** GI: Chris Huxley; **18-9:** GI: Darrell Gulin; **22:** GI: Darrell Gulin (b); **25:** GI: Darrell Gulin (b); **26-7, 28-9:** GI: Darrell Gulin (tc); **30:** GI: Darrell Gulin (t); **33:** GI: Darrell Gulin (t); **36-7:** GI: Photodisc; **40:** alamy.com: Dan Duchars (b); **43:** alamy.com: Dan Duchars (t); **44:** alamy.com: Dan Duchars (r); **47, 48:** alamy.com: Dan Duchars; **51:** alamy.com: Dan Duchars (b); **54-5:** Corbis: Craig Tuttle; **56-7:** GI: Rick Etkin; **57** GI: Andrew Hall (cr), James Darell (bl); **58:** Corbis: Craig Tuttle (r); **61:** Corbis: Craig Tuttle (r); **62-3, 66-7:** Corbis: Craig Tuttle; **70-1:** EWA; **73:** GI: James Day (bl); **74:** EWA; **76-77:** EWA (t); **78, 81, 82, 85:** EWA; **88-89:** NT: Alasdiar Ogilvie; **90:** alamy.com: Gondwana Photo Art (cl); **90-91:** Photonica: IPS; **91:** GI/Digital Vision (cr), EWA (bc); **93:** NT: Alasdiar Ogilvie; **94:** NT: Alasdiar Ogilvie (bl); **97:** NT: Alasdiar Ogilvie (br); **99:** NT: Alasdiar Ogilvie (tr); **103:** NT: Alasdiar Ogilvie (br); **106-107:** GI: John Dominis; **108:** alamy.com: Popperfoto (cl); **109:** GI: Karan Kapoor (cr); **111:** GI: John Dominis (b); **113:** GI: John Dominis; **114:** GI: John Dominis (b); **116:** GI:

John Dominis (t); **119:** GI: John Dominis; **120:** GI: John Dominis (t); **124-25:** GI: Photodisc; **126:** ImageState/ Picture: Age Fotostock (bl); **126-27:** Masterfile UK: Tom Collicott (t); **127:** GI: Chris Craymer (bc); **128:** GI: Chris Huxley; **131:** GI: Chris Huxley (tr); **132:** GI: Chris Huxley (tr); **135:** GI: Chris Huxley (br); **136:** GI: Chris Huxley (tr); **139:** GI: Chris Huxley (br); **142-43:** GI: Ed Freeman; **144-45:** alamy.com: Juliette Wade; **144:** GI: Art Wolfe (bc); Julie Toy (cl); **145:** GI: Ray Massey (br); **146:** Jerry Harpur: Marcus Harpur: RHS Chelsea 1996, Van Hale (b); **149:** Jerry Harpur: Marcus Harpur: RHS Chelsea 1996, Van Hale (b); **153:** Jerry Harpur: Marcus Harpur: RHS Chelsea 1996, Van Hale (b); **154:** Jerry Harpur: Marcus Harpur: RHS Chelsea 1996, Van Hale (t); **157:** Jerry Harpur: Marcus Harpur: RHS Chelsea 1996, Van Hale (t); **160-61:** Corbis: Art Underground; **162-63:** GI: Serge Krouglikoff; **164:** Corbis: Art Underground; **167:** Corbis: Art Underground (bl); **168:** Corbis: Art Underground (bl); **171:** Corbis: Art Underground (tr); **172:** Corbis: Art Underground (tr); **175:** Corbis: Art Underground; **178-79:** GI: Siegfried Layda; **180:** alamy.com: ImageState (cl); **180:** GI: Ghislain & Marie David de Lossy (bc); **180-81:** GI: Carin Krasner; **181:** Masterfile UK: Zoran Milich (cr); **182:** GI: Siegfried Layda (tc); **185:** GI: Siegfried Layda (bc); **189:** GI: Siegfried Layda (bc); **190:** GI: Siegfried Layda (bl); **192:** GI: Siegfried Layda (bl); **196-197:** GI: Ryan Mcvay; **198:** GI: Tony Garcia (cl); **198-99:** GI: Reza Estakhrian; **201:** GI: Ryan Mcvay; **203:** GI: Ryan Mcvay (tr); **204:** GI: Ryan Mcvay (br); **206:** GI: Ryan Mcvay (tr); **211:** GI: Ryan Mcvay (br); **214-15, 218, 221:** GI: Angela Wyant; **222:** GI: Angela Wyant (t); **225:** GI: Angela Wyant (b); **226:** GI: Angela Wyant; **229:** GI: Angela Wyant (b).

All other images © Dorling Kindersley
For further information see: www.dkimages.com